Shots

The Diminutive Guide to a Little Big Drink

ERIKKA HAA

BARNES
&NOBLE
BOOKS
NEW YORK

TO SHAWN O'FARRELL

This edition published by Barnes & Noble, Inc.
by arrangement with Quirk Packaging, Inc.
2003 Barnes & Noble

ISBN 0-7607-4765-2

Designed by Lynne Yeamans
Styling by Janet Prusa

Printed in China
M 10 9 8 7 6 5 4 3 2

Alcohol lowers the inhibitions and depresses the CNS—and lots of silly, and occasionally
stupid, behavior results. The author and publishers encourage you to keep it silly, and
avoid stupid. This publication contains the ideas and opinions of its author, and is designed
to provide useful information on alcoholic beverages and shot recipes to the reader.
Any references to products do not imply or constitute endorsement or recommendation.
The publisher and author neither endorse nor encourage the illegal or irresponsible
manufacture, sale, or use of such beverages, and specifically disclaim responsibility for
any liability, loss, damage, or injury allegedly arising from any information, recipe, or
suggestion in this book. DRINK RESPONSIBLY.

ACKNOWLEDGMENTS

In addition to the peerless staff at Quirk Packaging, David and Tanya Hughes of Hotfoot Studio, and stylist Janet Prusa, without whom this book would not be possible, many thanks go to the following for their invaluable friendship and support: Laura Cangelosi, Sarasun Cangelosi, MaryBeth Curley, Bill Doares, Nicole Fix and Karen Hartman, Roger Franz, Phil Friello, Simone Lee, Nathaniel Marunas, and Tara Shimandle—with special thanks as well to the countless bartenders and amateur mixologists who have at times risked life and limb in dauntless pursuit of the perfect potable.

Contents

Bartender's Tips

AN INTRODUCTION TO MIXOLOGY

Reminds me of my safari in Africa. Somebody forgot the corkscrew, and for several days we had to live on nothing but food and water.

—W. C. Fields

AS EVERY GOOD TRAVELER KNOWS, it's always wise to pack properly before the start of any trip, be it long or short. Same goes for getting the best out of most drink recipes—start out with the right equipment, and your adventures in alcohol should be absolutely smashing. And when it comes to shots, you can pack light.

Aside from the most obvious and barest of supplies, i.e., a bottle of booze and a couple of shot glasses, some basics worth acquiring include: a short or tall shaker, or both (a short shaker holds eight fluid ounces, half that of a regular tall shaker, but comes in very handy for its smaller size, especially when paired with a rocks glass); control pourers, at least two to four, perhaps a set of six (a must for layered shooters especially, lest more liquor end up on the counter rather than in the glasses); and the aforementioned rocks glasses, for those preferring their shots on ice (basically a double-shot glass, holding four to five fluid ounces, depending upon the maker, and the densest glass behind the bar). I leave the number of shot and rocks glasses up to you, as surely the best judge of the size of your own gatherings.

To round out a more complete cocktail repertoire you might want to add a couple of things: no bar would be complete, for example, without its very own "charmer," or basic wine bottle-opening device, consisting of an all-in-one corkscrew, bottle opener, and foil remover. (Very sexy, for a bar tool.) While most shots require no garnish—other than more alcohol—a sharp paring knife is worth having around simply because it is well designed for a specific purpose, and because you never know when a fresh fruit (a lemon or lime especially) may be called for. And wherever there's a sharp paring knife there ought to be a good quality cutting board. Finally, for those of more exacting sensibilities, a double-headed measuring jigger (of one and two ounces) is a perfect (not to mention cheap) addition to any aspiring mixmaster's collection.

As for technique, it's often best to keep it simple. Shooters are the simplest, poured straight-up—"neat" or "down." Shots over ice, or "on the rocks," are also easy, and you'll need the rocks glass. Next in difficulty may be layered shooters, though it really depends upon how steady your hands are. First, always pour following the order of liquors as provided in the recipe—the spirits will layer according to their densities, and will set properly only if you follow the correct order. After the first layer, pour each subsequent one slowly (this is where you'll be grateful for investing in control pourers, as that stopper hole will come in very handy here). One method is to pour the liquid over an inverted teaspoon, its edge flush with the inside of the shot glass. (I've found that an eyedropper works quite efficiently, though this technique might be better reserved for those of you with separate, or at least partially enclosed kitchens or home bars; one could hardly appear less suave than when wielding an eyedropper together with a bottle of booze.)

As a general rule, straight-up vodka, gin, and especially Jägermeister are at their finest when ice-cold, and should be stored in the freezer whenever possible, while Scotch and whiskey, brandy, rum, and most liqueurs (except for Irish cream) are perfectly suited for the back bar or household liquor cabinet. For shaken shots, it really doesn't matter whether your liquor comes straight from the freezer or has been loafing around at room temp, as you'll be throwing ice into the mix regardless.

SOME BASIC THINGS TO KEEP IN MIND WHILE SHAKING IT UP:

- Always put the ice in first—it will take up half the volume of your shaker, an important factor to remember whenever measuring ingredients for shaken shots or cocktails.
- Make sure you have a good grip (one hand on top and one on bottom) on your shaker before setting it in motion—especially on that little cap on top. (Unless you were already planning to redecorate the kitchen and buy your guests new clothes, of course.)
- A short shaker and rocks glass were made for each other—in fact, a short shaker fits over a rocks glass as perfectly as its taller version fits over a pint-size mixing glass, with both forming a vacuum-tight seal. A Kamikazi is among the better examples of this perfect union in action, as it can be built right in the rocks glass over a couple of ice cubes, covered and short shaken, then either served right back up in the same glass as a Kamikazi on the rocks, or strained neat into a couple of regular shot glasses.

And that's all for now, folks. Master these few simple basics, and you'll be well on your way to party central!

The Right Shot for the Job

Some shots are better than others at certain kinds of mood adjustment, whether you're looking for an after-work mood-booster shot or a dim-the-lights-and-let's-get-it-on quickie. The following key makes it easier to select the appropriate shot for the moment.

MOOD-LIGHTENERS: Look for this icon when it's time to get the party started. It's happy hour, and you need a drink that can make the problems of the day disappear—and get your mood adjusted for a good time.

OBLITERATORS: Watch out! This is one-shot shopping at its finest. These shots pack a wallop, and are perfect for when you need to get the festivities rolling fast. They may look benign, but don't underestimate their effect.

MEDICINAL: Shots that cure whatever ails you. Sometimes you need a quick pick-me-up, other times a good, stiff shock to the system is called for. These elixirs will have you feeling better in no time.

APHRODISIACS: Everyone knows about the dandiness of candy versus liquor's speed. Try one of these lust-inducing libations to get in the mood for love but fast.

Dragon's Breath, see page 13

A Shot in the Dark Ages

When alchemists first learned how to distill spirits, they called it *aqua vitae*, the "water of life," and far from considering it the work of the devil, they thought the discovery was divinely inspired.

—Gene Logsdon, *Good Spirits*

BETWEEN THE FALL OF THE ROMAN EMPIRE AND THE MIDDLE AGES, circa AD 500–1000, is a period of marked decline in the civilization of mankind. For Europe, the Dark Ages brought instability and disease, brutality and despair. In AD 535, a massive volcanic eruption in Southeast Asia spurred calamitous climate change across the known world. Ancient records report that for at least fifteen years seasons blurred while an anemic sun was often barely visible through dark and turbulent clouds. The bubonic plague made its first appearance only seven years later, overrunning Constantinople in AD 542.

Those kinds of conditions could drive anybody to drink—a lot. And since the available water was often unfit for consumption, only beer, wine, and mead were considered safe to drink. While the art of fermenting grains and grapes was already thousands of years old by this time, distillation (which seems to have originated in China before the eighth century) was still in its relative infancy, the finer points of the complicated process not yet fully understood.

Although much was lost in the dark days, some practical knowledge remained. Monasteries, which sustained winemaking through the ages, also developed many sweetened liqueurs, including Benedictine (1510), Chartreuse, and Frangelico. The seemingly miraculous properties of the ancient wormwood plant *(Artemisia absinthium)*, which acted as a vermifuge—it killed the intestinal worms that were a scourge at all levels of society—led to a wormwood-infused wine, the Bavarian *vermutwein*. It outlasted the Dark Ages to become one of the very first preprandial— before dinner—cordials.

Humble *vermutwein*'s lineage goes all the way back to *vinum Hippocraticum*, the legendary "wine of Hippocrates" (c. 460–377 BC). The ancient Romans drank *absinthianum vinum,* a direct descendant of Hippocrates' wormwood wine. Vermutwein eventually became *vermout,* described in 1678 as an aid to digestion and purifier of the blood, that "induces sound slumber" and "rejoices the heart."

Today we call it vermouth, that ancient apéritif and current member of the larger class of spirits known collectively as liqueurs, interchangeably as cordials. Other historic cordials include Amaretto (1525), Grand Marnier, Drambuie (1746), sambuca, and schnapps. From Germany comes the noble Jägermeister.

Dragon's Breath

FACE THE DRAGON...if you dare!

Crème de almond
Bailey's Irish Cream
Jägermeister

Layer in equal parts—and watch the Dragon's mighty breath rise as mist over the loch when it hits the Bailey's.

HAVE NO DOUBT, this is a thick, syrupy shot, with Jäger's spirited punch giving way to the doubly sweet dose of crème and cream. Cordials, by traditional definition, are sweeter than liquors, as they must contain at least $2^{1}/_{2}$ percent sugar by weight—many, however, are much sweeter, containing up to 35 percent sugar. Crèmes are found most often among the sweeter set and crème de almond is no exception. Despite its name, crème de almond is often made from a distillate of apricot kernels, while its kissing cousin, crème de noyaux, is produced primarily by distilling the oil of bitter almonds. There's nothing bitter about Bailey's, however, an exceptionally smooth liqueur made with cream, some chocolate, eggs, and Irish whiskey.

Jägermeister

STEP 1: Remove pre-chilled, distinctive square bottle of Jägermeister from freezer.

STEP 2: Measure one jiggerful mysterious herb-infused potion from Germany.

STEP 3: Knock back vigorously; allow warmth to fill chest and lighten head; feel aches melt to memories and worries slip away.

WHENCE THIS FRAGRANT BALM TO HUMANITY? In the seventh century, according to the Jägermeister legend, Prince Hubertus, despondent over the sudden death of his princess, Floribana, turned his back on his fellow royals, and went in search of abject solitude. While on one of his many lone hunting trips in the deep black forests of Germany, Hubertus was beguiled by an enormous stag with what appeared to be a holy cross floating between its antlers (prompting one to wonder which came first: the Jägermeister or the deer). Moved by this vision to give up his title and all his material possessions, Hubertus founded several monasteries (the monastery-cum-brewery tradition was already venerable even then, prompting one to wonder again which came first: the monk or the malt) and became the Patron Saint of Hunters after his death.

What is Liqueur?

HOW SWEET IT IS!

HOW DID A SUBSTANCE SO SIMPLY DEFINED—a sweetened alcoholic beverage with a neutral-spirit base (often brandy) flavored with the infusion of fruit, herbs, nuts, seeds, or spices—achieve such a historically pivotal position? For the answer we have to look way back into humankind's history, and to our understanding of mortality.

Medieval alchemists believed there were natural elixirs yet to be discovered that could—despite the obvious evidence to the contrary—lead to eternal life. Ridiculous? Perhaps, though certainly no farther-fetched than their dream of turning metal into gold. In comparison, the alchemists' quest for that ever-elusive immortality was really rather down to earth. Quite literally, in fact, as we must look back again to the monastery with its religiously tended gardens and vineyards to find the very first liqueurs.

Considering its lineage, it's hardly surprising that early attempts at distillation produced beverages that were downright awful, or that monks in their monasteries began infusing these spirits with all manner of barks, berries, flowers, nuts, and roots to try to make the stuff more palatable. After drawing off the fruit-steeped liquor following this infusion, a sweetened syrup was often added, proving that a spoonful of sugar really does "make the medicine go down." Consuming these concoctions rounded the edges, thereby softening the burden of mortality. Life may still be short, but oh how sweet it can be!

Lights Out

IF YOU START hearing drums, it might be a good idea just to head home.

Vodka

Jägermeister

Shake well with ice or layer 2 parts vodka to 1 part Jägermeister—either way it's... I think you get the picture.

 "LAST CALL," OR "TAPS"—a last bugle call blown to signal lights out on military bases—originated from a corruption of the Dutch phrase *tap toe*, meaning "taps shut." This was the call that went out at closing time to turn off the beer spigots and shut out the lights at many waterfront taverns. The tradition is also called a "Last Post" when preceded by a drummer's "tattoo" (another variation on *tap toe*, also referred to as *taptoo*). In the early 19th century, an orderly sergeant would accompany the regimental drummer as he marched through a post beating the "Tattoo" to signal the end of the day—only upon reaching the last barracks would "Taps" be sounded (this is the reason military drummers traditionally carried bugles as well).

Alaskan Oil Slick

THIS PARTICULAR SHOT may indeed resemble something of an oil spill over the deep blue sea—and its icy cold bite could make you wonder why you were ever worried about going down with the ship.

Blue curaçao
Rumple Minze Peppermint Schnapps
Jägermeister

Layer in equal parts.

THERE MAY NOT BE ENOUGH ROOM IN YOUR FREEZER FOR THAT MANY BOTTLES, but try to keep the Jägermeister and Rumple Minze, at the very least, ice-cold—they make excellent shooters on their own, and are best served straight from the freezer (the liquid's viscosity will rise, but the alcohol content will prevent these liqueurs from solidifying). Imported from Germany's Scharlachberg Distillery, Rumple Minze is self-described as the "original peppermint schnapps," and at 100 proof, it's as potent as it is minty. Because of the higher alcohol content, Rumple Minze is also not as syrupy-sweet as your average schnapps, which are usually in only the 40–60 proof range. Shot straight up and ice-cold, the sharp, clear, and clean taste of mint is surprisingly fresh, with "natural" as opposed to "flavored" tones—followed by a wallop of hard alcohol. The blue curaçao is added primarily for its color, but the subtle orange flavor adds a nice, light touch.

Black Gold

THE LIQUEURS FOR THIS SHOT ARE FAIRLY COOPERATIVE and will form two distinct layers that remain clearly separated. All that glitters is not guileless, however, as this is a pretty little shot that packs a serious punch!

Jägermeister
Goldschläger

Layer in equal parts.

DRUNKEN STORIES ABOUND AND GATHER THICKLY AROUND THE PRINCELY GOLDSCHLÄGER, with a general consensus swirling about the fact that this Swiss schnapps definitely "sneaks up on you"—with more than one hapless victim confessing, "I've never been reduced to a state like that in my life." Indeed. Basically a strong, cinnamon-flavored schnapps, Goldschläger gets its name (and part of its rollicking reputation) from the 23K gold-leaf flakes added to the liqueur—give the bottle a good shake and you've got a snow globe for grown-ups (albeit grown-ups destined to be reduced to childish babbling if they're not careful). Rumor has it those gold flecks, despite being undetectable on the way down, may serve a purpose beyond their glinting good looks.

Bob Marley

YOU, TOO, could be jammin'.

Jägermeister
Goldschläger
Midori

Layer in equal parts.

YOU WON'T END UP WITH RASTA COLORS, exactly, but the addition of mellow Midori helps put the "chill" in "chill out"—softening Jägermeister's herbally infused and medicinal bite while rounding the edges of Goldschläger's spicy cinnamon sting. And this American melon liqueur has just the right résumé for the job: Midori made its debut in 1978 at none other than New York's legendary Studio 54, according to the company bio. At the center of party central, the subtly sweet, light yet luscious emerald-green liqueur quickly became a favorite of the cocktail crowd, and won the coveted first prize at the U.S. Bartender's Guild Annual Cocktail Championship that same year (for the Melon Ball and Sex on the Beach). Perhaps a tad too sweet for the macho solo shooter, Midori appeals to more modest drinkers who prefer their slammers fruity rather than flammable. Midori also makes for an excellent and colorful mixer in cocktails and shots alike with its amiable ability to take the edge off the stronger spirits it often finds itself sharing a glass with.

A Short Snort

THE WEE DRAM

IN THE TIME OF WILLIAM THE CONQUEROR (1027–1087), the good bishop Wulstan was "obliged to maintain a large retinue of men-at-arms, as the Danes were daily expected," according to spirits historian Gene Logsdon. Over the long hours his soldiers spent drinking, "[Wulstan] would keep them company to restrain them by his presence, pledging them when it came his turn in a tiny cup, which he pretended to taste, and in the midst of the din ruminating to himself on the psalms." Much later, bartenders at the height of the saloon era in North America would employ a similar method to avoid getting too high on their own supplies—the savvier "bardog" kept a private "snit" behind his bar that he used when many a customer insisted he buy himself a drink.

As for the origins of shot, or *scot*, meaning "payment," it's back to the Middle Ages. Halfway through the thirteenth century, the private drinking parties known as "scot-ales" came under fire from the Church. A decree was issued against the practice (in which participants arrived at a predetermined location and paid for drinks there) but the clerical habit of announcing the next scot-ale—in church—made the enforcement of the decree difficult, to say the least. Instead, the parties swiftly proliferated and grew to include "help-ales"—for the party thrower in debt—and "bride-ales"—for the young medieval couple just starting out.

Rumple Meister

You may think you've mastered the Rumple, but the Rumple is always master.

Jägermeister
Rumple Minze Peppermint Schnapps

Layer equal parts Jägermeister and Rumple Minze...and let the wild rumpus begin!

EVEN IF ONLY IN A DREAM, it's good to be king or queen of the pack for a night. Before donning that wolf suit, however, it's prudent to remember that overly rambunctious behavior could get you unceremoniously tossed from the bar. Here are some simple guidelines, from an anonymous definition of drunkenness:

He is not drunk who from the floor
Can rise again and drink once more.
But he is drunk who prostrate lies
And cannot drink and cannot rise.

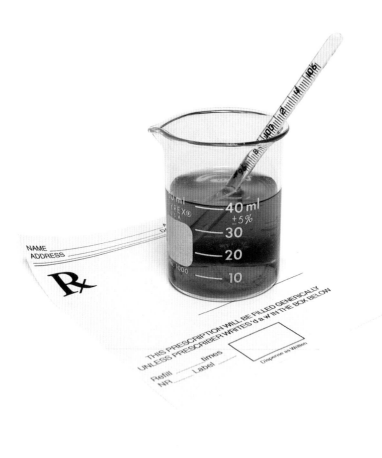

Nitequell, see page 29

Take Your Medicine

There are more old drunkards than there are old doctors.

—Old pub proverb

THE MISTY ORIGINS OF WHAT WE CALL "VODKA" TODAY began with its development (possibly by an Arab alchemist) as early as the eighth century. At first it was used for purely medicinal purposes. Perhaps owing to its versatility—it can be produced from a variety of plants, including grains such as rye and wheat, as well as beets, potatoes, and molasses—vodka became especially popular in Eastern Europe, where the plants from which it could be distilled adapted well to a northern climate. Used exclusively for its "healing" properties until at least the 1400s, it was believed that this *aqua vitae* could strengthen the body and prolong life, according to French alchemist Arnaud de Villeneuve. Hence vodka's long reign over the pervasive and centuries-old tradition of drinkers toasting to one another's health.

Before the art of distillation came to Europe from the East, the process of fermentation set naturally low limits on the amount of ethyl alcohol that could be produced. If you wanted a stronger drink, you had to further ferment your wine or beer, allow it to freeze, then draw off the more concentrated alcoholic slush that formed while it thawed. Distillation blew the lid off all that, further breaking down an already-fermented and alcoholic brew to its purer, far more potent essence. The greater concentration that the distillation process afforded simply raised the alcoholic content of whatever didn't boil off.

Sounds easy, doesn't it? But of course nothing is ever really that simple, and distillation is no exception. The art lies in the understanding that different liquids—depending on their composition, among other factors—reach their boiling points at different temperatures. It should also come as no surprise that the perfection of such an art would be attempted by many masters. So it is that Russia and Poland both lay claim to the invention of vodka as their very own. The name itself is derived from the Russian *zhiznennaia voda*, or "water of life" (harking back again to the Latin), which was later shortened to *voda* (vodka means "little water"). In Poland (and Germany) vodka—originally known as *okowita*, another derivation of *aqua vitae*—is called *wodka*, short for and adapted from *zhiznennaia voda*.

The historical record points to both Poland *and* Russia's familiarity with vodka as early as the twelfth century. Commercial production of Polish vodka was attained by the fourteenth or fifteenth century (with Sweden not far behind), while the state took over vodka producton in Russia, setting up a monopoly that lasted centuries.

Nitequell

Inspired by—but much more delicious than—the famous "sniffling, sneezing, coughing, aching, stuffy-head, fever so you can rest medicine" and you don't need to be fighting a cold to try it.

Vodka
Blue curaçao
Green crème de menthe

Shake well with ice 2 parts vodka to 1 part each blue curaçao and green crème de menthe.

TAKE TWO OF THESE—and for goodness' sake don't call me in the morning. Wait until noon, at least.

Eastern Europe abounds with homegrown vodka-based cold and flu remedies. In Armenia, for example, one such remedy resembles something of a "vodka body shot"—call it "Vodka Rub": simply rub straight vodka onto the sufferer's chest. Another popular cold cure calls for adding as much ground pepper as you can stand to a shot of vodka—then shoot back while still swirling, hit the sack, and "wake up cured."

Vodka

RAISE THAT VODKA SLOWLY TO YOUR LIPS AND SUDDENLY: SPARKS!
They fly from your stomach to the furthest reaches of your body.

—Anton Chekhov, *The Siren*

NEAT, CLEAN, AND CRISP: 1¹/₂ ounces of satin elegance—with bite. Never mind the drink-vodka-martinis-and-they'll-never-know-you-had-three-for-lunch myth—perpetuated by years of wishful thinking—for while some vodkas are certainly smoother than others, all are definitively hard alcohol, and proudly show it.

And why not? It's tradition, after all. Few toasts are as steeped in ritual and custom—as unparalleled in their sociability—as are those that include the raising of the venerable vodka shot. In Russia, one of many cultures of which it can be said, "To drink is to be festive, to be festive is to drink," a shot of vodka is proffered in celebration of everything from a christening to a graduation, a wedding, or a birth. Best served ice-cold straight from the freezer, a shot of vodka is to Scandinavian Christmas what a Mint Julep is to the Kentucky Derby. For New Year's Day in Denmark, getting off on the right foot often means having a "first foot": Upon arrival in celebration of a new year's dawning, guests may be greeted at the door with a first nip—a shot of vodka, cold and clear as a Nordic winter.

Bottoms Up!

Merry met and merry part
I drink to you with all my heart!

SHOULD YOU EVER TRAVEL AROUND THE WORLD WITHOUT A PLAN, you'll never be lonely with a glass in hand, for the list below will help you raise a toast "To Your Health!" in many a foreign land:

Belgium: Op uw gezonheid

Brazil/Spain: Salud

China: Wen lie

Denmark/Norway/Sweden: Sköl

Egypt: Fee sihetak

Finland: Kippis

France: A votre santé

Germany: Prosit

Greece: Yasas

Hawaii: Kamau

Holland: Proost

Hungary: Ege' sze' ge' rel

Iceland: Santaka nu

India: Aap ki shubh kai liyai

Ireland: Sláinte

Italy: Alla saluté

Japan: Kanpei

Korea: Konbe

North America/England/Australia: Cheers

Pakistan: Sanda bashi

Poland: Na zdrowie

Portugal: A sua saude

Russia: Nas zdarovia

Scotland: Hoot mon

Singapore: Yam seng

South Africa: Oogy wawa

Taiwan: Gun bi

Thailand: Chai yo

Turkey: Serefe

Gin

Vodka

Tabasco sauce

Build with gin and vodka right in the shot glass—never mind the layering, just shoot for equal parts, with a little room left over—then top off with a dash of Tabasco sauce (or your own fiery favorite)…and it's not out of the frying pan but straight into the fire for you!

ANOTHER HOMESPUN CURE, centuries old, revolves around the hot chili pepper, highly prized in this context as a powerful expectorant. In Russia, vodka and chilies are combined to make *nastoyka*—simply add a pod or two of red or green chili peppers to a bottle of straight vodka and let it sit for a day or so.

Also used for treating rheumatism as well as some causes of stomach distress (except, of course, ulcers), *nastoyka* is often served as an aperitif among heartier souls. Whew! That'll certainly clear the sinuses!

Antarctica

THE SKYY'S the limit.

Blue curaçao
Vodka (ice-cold)

Layer in equal parts.

 I SUGGEST USING ONE OF THE PREMIUM VODKAS FOR THIS SHOT, as a lesser product could get lost in the curaçao. Skyy, with its quadruple distillation process and three-step filtration system is perfect for the job. Made in the U.S.A. since 1993, Skyy was declared "one of the hottest spirit brands" by *Impact* magazine. Store the Skyy in the freezer and keep the blue curaçao in the fridge (this citrus liqueur is thick enough as it is, freezing will only raise the viscosity), if possible, as the lower the liquid temperature the better for this cooler shooter. Citrus liqueurs were fairly common by the ninth century, especially in Spain. Originally named for the Caribbean island of Curaçao where it was first produced, curaçao has become a generic appellation for a low-proof liqueur flavored with the bitter oil extracted from the dried peel of any variety of orange. Popular in a wide variety of cocktails and shooters for its subtle yet straight-up flavor, curaçao also arrives at the party dressed in green, orange, or clear, with only slight variations in bitterness.

Emerald Isle

Here's to health and prosperity,
To you and all your posterity.
And them that doesn't drink with sincerity,
That they may be damned for all eternity!

—Irish toast

Midori
Blue curaçao
Vodka

Pour equal parts of each, and shake well with ice.

THINK GREEN: if you want to stay true to this shot's emerald theme, try tracking down Boru, a handcrafted, quadruple-distilled *Irish* vodka—a rare gem indeed. This vodka is named for Brian Boru (c. 940–1014), who drove out the Vikings and became the first high king of Ireland. Boru is the brainchild of the people behind Bailey's Irish Cream. The high production standards at the Carbery Distillers in Ringsend are evident in this vodka's crisp, clean taste—it's made with natural spring water and filtered through Irish oak. They may not stock Boru at your local liquor store, but it is available.

Gin & Sin

Little nips of whiskey,
Little drops of gin,
Make a lady wonder
Where on earth she's bin'

—Anonymous

GIN IS NEARLY INDISTINGUISHABLE FROM VODKA IN EVERY WAY EXCEPT ONE—flavor (though some vodka loyalists still maintain that gin is merely flavored vodka). Gin can be colorless, but it is hardly odorless or free of taste, as its elder, vodka, is often described. Gin arrived late to the party, its origin most often attributed to Franciscus Sylvius (a.k.a. Franciscus de le Boë), a professor of medicine at Holland's University of Leiden. In the seventeenth century, Sylvius produced an inexpensive medicinal diuretic by distilling the oil of juniper berries together with grain alcohol. Too bitter to eat raw, the bluish-black berries, native to Europe and North America, were generally dried and used to flavor meats and sauces. In fact, the French had already been using the essence of juniper berries to flavor their "poor wines" in an effort to make the stuff more palatable. The Dutch in turn adopted the French word for the juniper berry, *genièvre*, to name Holland's increasingly popular "medicinal" tonic. It was later called *genever* and then *geneva*, and shortened by the English to simply *gin*.

During the brutally long campaigns of the Thirty Years' War (1618–1648), British troops fighting beside the Dutch were given gin to combat the often-debilitating cold and damp of the Low Countries (Belgium, Luxembourg, and the Netherlands). Duly impressed by not only the warming qualities of this unknown liquor but also the fighting spirit of their allies, the Brits nick-named gin "Dutch Courage" and

1862: The Martini is born. Originally called a "Martinez," it consists of 4 parts *sweet* vermouth to 1 part gin, with a cherry garnish.

brought it home with them to England, where it quickly caught on.

In 1689, William III, Prince of Orange and ruler of Holland, ascended the British throne through his marriage to Mary, daughter of King James II. During the reign of William and Mary the king actively encouraged the mass production of gin, allowing a distiller to set up shop a mere ten days after posting a public notice. The heavily sweetened and inexpensive "Old Tom's Gin" was especially popular with the poor, and "Mother's Milk" became "Mother's Ruin" as abuse ran rampant. By 1730, there were more than 7,000 dramshops in London alone, according to several sources.

The Gin Act of 1736 sought to gain a handle on an out-of-control situation by raising taxes and limiting licenses, but the ensuing riots and illicit (and often deadly) production of "gin," using anything from beer-mash dregs to rotten vegetables, led to the act's repeal in 1742. Cooler heads eventually prevailed, consumption fell, and the quality of gin had vastly improved by the time "London Dry" was introduced in the 1870s.

Machs I, II, and III

EVER DREAM OF BREAKING THE SOUND BARRIER but not quite ready to join the Air Force? Try this aerodynamic trio on for size.

Gin
Fresh lemonade
Green chartreuse
Black sambuca

MACH I: Start by seeing whether you've got the right stuff. Try this simple, layered shot of gin and lemonade, equal parts.

MACH II: To reach the next level, you're going to need a tall shot glass. Layer green chartreuse, gin, and lemonade in equal amounts. And fasten your seatbelt.

MACH III: Watch that altimeter and prepare to engage autopilot: Layer equally black sambuca, green chartreuse, gin, and lemonade. If you can't feel your ears popping by now, you're already unconscious.

 A LITTLE-KNOWN FACT about legendary navigator Christopher Columbus's pioneering quest to find a shorter passage to the East Indies by sailing westward across the Atlantic is that it was initially planned in the Chartreux monastery of Sevilla, Spain, with help from a Chartreux father.

Goin' Down Easy

THESE SHOTS ARE GOOD FOR WHAT AILS YOU—easy to prepare (no more than 2 ingredients), and easy to get down. You'll feel better soon, I promise!

 YOU KNOW THOSE DAYS WHEN YOU NEED A SOLID DRINK, but the thought of sipping a whole gin and tonic or bottle of beer is just too much? Those are usually the same days when enduring the kick from whiskey might force you into early retirement. These shots are the best of both worlds: short, strong, and easy on the digestive sysem.

Misty Mountaintop

Vodka
Irish Mist

Start with equal parts any straight vodka and Irish Mist—pour as a straight-up shooter or shake well with ice and strain, whatever your pleasure—then simply sit back and enjoy the view!

Silver Bullet

Vodka
Sambuca

Shake equal parts vodka and sambuca well with ice and strain. An anise-flavored and gently stimulating liqueur, sambuca is named for the ancient elderberry *(Sambuscus canadensis)* from which it is derived. Folklore holds that the elderberry, a member of the honeysuckle family, can provide protection from evil as well as ward off witches, and across Europe and parts of Russia it is still considered good luck to serve sambuca at both weddings and wakes.

Grapes of Bath

Gin
Purple grape juice

If you're in the mood for a shot of gin, mix yourself a nice, dry Martini. But if you're looking for a little fun with your gin, try a splash of grape juice with your juniper. Stick with a London Dry (preferably ice-cold), if possible, lest you end up with a serious clash of the berries, and build your purple potable right in the glass, either equal parts gin and juice or 2-to-1. For a taller shooter, top it off with a dash of ginger ale, for something of a variation on a Moscow Mule (originally vodka and ginger beer, later switched to ginger ale).

Kamikazi

AS CLASSIC A COCKTAIL as it is a consummate shooter.

Vodka
Rose's lime juice
Triple sec

STEP 1: If you have a short shaker, you can make both cocktail and shooter with one glass: Pour about 1¼ oz. (a standard-size shot) straight vodka over ice in a rocks glass, followed by about 1 oz. each Rose's lime juice and triple sec.

STEP 2: Now cover and shake up that rocks glass.

STEP 3: If your guest wants a sipper, simply break the shaker's seal and gently pour the now icy tipple right back into the rocks glass, ice and all. For a couple of 2-oz. shooters, just break it and strain it.

 THE SHORT SHAKER AND ROCKS GLASS were made for each other, and no other potable, in my book, takes better advantage of that perfect union, with one caveat—the Kamikazi earned its reckless reputation from the fact that it tastes way too good, with an icy sweet-and-sour tang that can make you forget you're drinking anything like alcohol…or where you live…how you got here from there…

Grand Slam

LIKE A GRAND SLAM (be it in bridge, golf, baseball, or any other sport), this shooter is a definite winner!

Grand Marnier Cordon Rouge
Tanqueray London Dry Gin
Orange juice
Grenadine
Cherry

STEP 1: Shake 1 part Grand Marnier, 2 parts Tanqueray, and 2 parts orange juice well with ice.

STEP 2: Strain into shot glasses—how many will depend on whether you shook it up tall or short—leaving just enough room for a splash of grenadine and a cherry garnish.

 THE GRAND MARNIER PUTS THE "GRAND" IN THIS SLAM, the Tanqueray keeps it regal, and the orange juice ensures this knockout's no slipped Mickey. Grand Marnier gets its distinctive flavor from orange peels used during the distillation process, which will be accentuated by the orange juice in this shot.

The Oyster

What decency does Venus observe when she is drunken? when she knows
not head from tail, eats giant oysters at midnight.

—Juvenal, *Satire VI*; translation by G. G. Ramsay

Vodka

Lemon juice

Worcester sauce

Horseradish

Salt and pepper

Fresh or smoked oyster

Just shake up a small batch of traditional Marys—a shot of vodka, dash of lemon
juice, 1/2 teaspoon Worcester sauce, pinch of horseradish, salt and pepper to
taste—strain into desired number of shot glasses, then add the oyster on the side.

 LIKE THE G-SPOT, some people prefer to think of aphrodisiacs as
mythical, but oysters really do have a claim to loosening the libido.
For one thing, they're packed with zinc, a deficiency of which can
cause impotence. Zinc also controls progesterone levels, which are
essential for a healthy sex drive. In addition, oysters contain dopamine, which
heightens sensation and awareness, both key elements in enhancing that special
evening, morning, lunch break...

Bourbon Street, see page 53

Down By Law

> If when you say "whiskey" you mean the devil's brew, the poison scourge, the bloody monster that defiles innocence, dethrones reason...then I am certainly against it. But, if when you say "whiskey" you mean the oil of conversation, the philosophic wine...the drink that enables a man to magnify his joy...then I am certainly for it. This is my stand. I will not retreat from it. I will not compromise.
>
> —Judge Noah Sweat

WHEN THE NORMANS INVADED IRELAND in the twelfth century, they encountered a proud and well-established tradition of distilling "usky" (a mispronunciation of *usquebaugh*). Both Emerald Islanders and Scottish Highlanders lay similar claims to inventing whisk(e)y (or "whisky," to Aussie, Britons, Canadians, Japanese, New Zealanders, and Scots.) At least one popular theory posits that the ancient Celts (ancestors of the Cornish, Irish, Scottish, and Welsh) were distilling grains as early as 800 BC. Another states that archeologists have found the basis of Scotch whiskey in fossil evidence of the prehistoric brews of the Picts and their ancestors—dating back to at least 2000 BC. The heather-flavored ales of the Picts would have been products of the fermentation of barley malt and grains—the primitive beer mash forming the basis of what would eventually become Scotch whiskey.

The Irish, for their part, may have learned the art of distillation from missionary monks in the seventh century. Some 200 years later Irish monks in turn arrived in Scotland—bringing their primitive whiskey-producing pot stills with them.

In Scotland, the first written reference to whiskey appeared in 1494, when "Eight bolls of malt to Friar John Cor wherewith to make aqua vitae" was listed in the Scottish Exchequer Rolls. Served as many as three times a day, often beginning before breakfast, whiskey was an integral part of Highland life—it kept out the cold and comforted the weary traveler; it disinfected wounds and tempered fevers; it acted as an anaesthetic during childbirth. Whiskey's medicinal status, for better or worse, was sealed in 1505 when the Guild of Surgeon Barbers in Edinburgh was granted a monopoly over its production—a process that holds the key to whiskey's distinction. Made primarily from malted barley, the mash is heated and infused with the fumes from a peat fire, giving Scotch whiskeys their uniquely smoky malt flavor. Today fine whiskeys are produced all across the globe, but by law only a whiskey made in Scotland can be labeled "Scotch."

Whiskey arrvied in North America in the late 1700s, where its story continued to be marked by contradiction and controversy, tariff, and taxation.

**Beefsteak when I'm hungry,
Red liquor when I'm dry,
Greenbacks when I'm hard up,
And religion when I die.**

— **"Way Up on Clinch Mountain,"
traditional American folksong**

Bourbon whiskey
Amaretto

Pour straight up equal parts bourbon and amaretto.

NO SHAKING OR STIRRING NECESSARY, though doing the Mardi Gras Mambo before, perhaps not during, but definitely after this little party shooter is highly recommended. Just be careful which krewe you join with to celebrate Fat Tuesday.

While the official Carnival season, with its lavish balls and other colorful celebrations, begins on the Twelfth Night after Christmas and culminates on Mardi Gras, or the day before Ash Wednesday, which marks the start of Lent, the krewes' parades really get swinging only about two weeks before Fat Tuesday, with the grandest held the weekend before. Part of a proud New Orleans tradition since at least 1837, there are more than sixty krewes in operation today.

Boilermaker

Rye whiskey
Beer

Pour whiskey and shoot it, then drink beer.

COINED IN 1834 to describe the craftsmen who built and maintained the boilers of steam locomotives, "boilermaker" became the proper name for a "whiskey with a beer chaser" by 1865, according to *Webster's*. It was originally called the Shawn O'Farrell (presumably after one very thirsty immigrant miner) in its birthplace of Butte, Montana, where it was the copper miner's custom to knock back several after-work O'Farrells as soon as he could make it to the nearest watering hole. Another variation to the helper calls for pouring the shot of whiskey directly into an ice-cold mug of beer. For those desirous of somewhat more questionable entertainment (try explaining this one to your dentist), drop the shooter, glass and all, right into your pint glass, and you'll have the appropriately named Depth Charge—daringly downed in just one draught. For a Russian Boilermaker: substitute vodka for whiskey.

Canadian Mountie

Although the RCMP was founded partly to eliminate the whiskey trade (an early success was the 1875 shutting down of the notorious whiskey camp known as Fort Whoop-up, in southern Alberta), the Mounties are nevertheless commemorated with this polite yet potent shooter.

Yukon Jack Canadian Liqueur
Seagram's VO

Half a shot of each, straight up.

GENERALLY SMOOTHER AND LIGHTER than their American cousins, bourbon and rye, Canadian blended whiskeys are distilled strictly from the cereal grains, primarily corn, mixed with barley, rye, and wheat. Canadian whiskeys must be made in Canada, and must be aged at least three years, though most spend an average of four to six years in the wood. Yukon Jack, though often mistaken for one, isn't a whiskey at all, but a blend of whiskey and honey-based liqueur that is somewhat akin to triple sec and calls itself the "Black Sheep of Canadian Liqueurs."

Despite the Canadian Parliament's earlier efforts to abolish the whiskey trade, as well as the passing of the Volstead Act in the U.S. in 1919, which provided enforcement for the Eighteenth Amendment, in 1924 fully two-thirds of the whiskey imported into the States came across the border from Canada, according to the U.S. Coast Guard.

Whiskey Medley

BOURBON, CANADIAN, IRISH, TENNESSEE, RYE —there's a whiskey for every taste.

CANADIAN WHISKEY IS A BLEND; it is lighter in taste and color than bourbon. Maker's Mark bourbon differs from most in that it is aged in copper, rather than oak, barrels. Tennessee whiskey, like bourbon, comes from a 51 percent corn mash, but is charcoal-filtered. Irish whiskey is made from a mixture of fresh and malted barley. Rye whiskey is almost entirely malted rye.

Black Tooth

Canadian whiskey
Coca-Cola

Top off at least 2 parts Canadian whiskey with a healthy splash of Coca-Cola.

Heavy Metal Maker

Goldschläger
Maker's Mark Small-Batch Kentucky Bourbon

Layer ice-cold Goldschläger cinnamon schnapps and Maker's Mark equally.

Lynchburg Lemonade

Jack Daniel's Tennessee Whiskey
Lemon juice
Grenadine

Shake two parts Jack Daniel's, one part lemon juice, plus a splash of grenadine well with ice.

Dublin Doubler

Tullamore Dew Blended Irish Whiskey
Bailey's Irish Cream

Shake Tullamore Dew Blended Irish Whiskey and Bailey's Irish Cream well with ice, then strain into a shot glass or preferably two—and it's double the luck of the Irish for you!

The Cowboy

Wild Turkey Straight Rye Whiskey
Half-and-half

For that "high and lonesome" kind of feeling, shake two parts Wild Turkey and one part half-and-half well with ice.

The Angels' Share

ALCHEMY, n. a power or process of transforming something common into something special, especially aiming to achieve the transmutation of the base metals into gold, the discovery of a universal cure for disease, and the discovery of a means of indefinitely prolonging life.

—*Merriam-Webster's Collegiate Dictionary*

SO HOW DO YOU GET TO WHISKEY FROM BEER? Shake one part alchemy, two parts civilization's discontent, a hefty dose of humankind's hopes and fears, plus a magic bean or two—and don't forget the pixie dust, for good luck.

What's the matter, then? What, you don't have a thousand years to fiddle around with this stuff? Okay, let's start with the practical basics: distillation works on the principle that different liquids will reach their boiling points at different temperatures; the process separates a liquid's elemental components, then collects the condensation as the vapors are cooled (for example, fermented barley—liquid "beer mash"). The vapors, or "condensate," are then drawn off, and go on to one of two fates. They may be transferred to wooden casks or barrels for aging (which distinguishes "brown" spirits like whiskey) or they may be redistilled to achieve greater purity, the required proof, and/or to add distinctive flavorings, as with the unaged "white" spirits like vodka or gin.

The apparatus employed in this process is the still. The simplest of these is the pot still, which consists of a large copper-lined pot that is connected to a cooled spiral tube that acts as a condenser. The condenser in turn leads to the vapor-collecting compartment of the still. In 1826 an Irishman named Aeneas Coffey (1780–1852), who worked as a tax collector in Scotland, introduced the continuous still. Also called the column, patent, or Coffey still, it revolutionized the liquor industry, eliminating the need for separate redistillation by continuously recycling the alcoholic vapors until all of the desired spirit is extracted. While the continuous still did not replace the pot still, the mass production it allowed dramatically expanded the market for Scottish whiskey.

SPIRIT, n. any of certain subtle fluids formerly supposed to permeate the body or a substance and impart to it its peculiar properties; also, the essence or active principle of a substance as extracted in liquid form, especially by distillation.

—The New Century Dictionary

If it's meant to become whiskey, the raw, colorless stuff that emerges from these stills is sent straight to the wood (often charred oak barrels) for the long, mellowing process of aging. As natural wood is porous, these barrels tend to "breathe," and a good whiskey can lose up to nearly a third of its original volume in the process—offering to the heavens above its "Angels' Share."

Harley Davidson

PULL OVER, WHO'S DRIVING? Definitely not you—this ain't no scooter shooter. If you really want to get your motor running, live to ride another day—two wheels, three wheels, four wheels...steer clear of any kind of wheels after this (or any other) shot.

Jack Daniel's Tennessee Whiskey
Yukon Jack Canadian Liqueur
Lemon wedge

It's Jack on Jack, as in half Daniel's and half Yukon—a marriage of the Old South and the Great White North. Just pour straight up, shoot right back, then suck on a wedge of lemon to help you enjoy it going down.

JASPER NEWTON "JACK" DANIEL (1850–1911) bought his first still at the tender age of thirteen. In 1866, he registered his whiskey-making business with the government, making Jack Daniel's oldest registered distillery in the United States.

Another American classic, the Harley-Davidson Motor Company, was founded in 1903 by William S. Harley and Arthur Davidson. The company's first "factory" was nothing but a small wooden shed, and its first bike was built to race. And race it did—by 1920 Harley-Davidson was simply "the largest manufacturer of motor-cycles in the world."

Miles of Smiles

A SHOT AND A JOKE...a timeless combination.

White crème de menthe
Rye whiskey
Amaretto

Layer equal parts each.

THE CLASSIC BARROOM JOKE always begins the same way...

A man walks into a bar and hears piano music. He looks at the piano but can't see anyone sitting there, so he walks over and discovers a foot-tall man standing on the piano bench, playing the tune of "Dixie-Girl." The man thinks this is strange, so he goes over to the bartender and asks where the man came from.

"Here," says the bartender, handing the man a genie's lamp, "rub this."

"What do you wish for?" asks the genie.

"A million bucks," the man declares, quite sure of himself.

"Granted." And the genie claps his hands and disappears back into the lamp.

The man looks around, checks his wallet, but can't find a million bucks anywhere. Just then, a million ducks fly noisily through the bar. Astounded, the man exclaims, "Hey! I didn't ask for a million ducks!"

"Do you think I asked for a 12-inch pianist?" replies the bartender.

Bee Sting, see page 69

A Divine Madness

TEQUILA HAS NO HISTORY; there are no stories confirming its birth. This is how it has been since the beginning of time, for tequila is a gift from the gods, and they don't tend to offer fables when bestowing favors. That is the job of mortals, the children of panic and tradition.

—Alvaro Mutis, "Tequila: Panegyric and Emblem"; translation by Mark Schafer

FOR SOME 15,000 YEARS before the Spanish conquistadors arrived, people had been settling in what was to become Mexico. Civilizations eventually grew around the sustaining crop of this vast Central American region—maize—and by about 1000 BC Mexican agriculture was flourishing. At its height (approximately AD 301–900), the Mayan Empire covered the Yucatán peninsula and Belize as well as the state of Chiapas in southern Mexico, and extended into most of modern-day Guatemala, western El Salvador, and Honduras. The Mayas were primarily farmers, and grew beans, cassava, cotton, and sweet potatoes as well as corn. Accomplished apiarists, they kept bees for wax and honey. While the complex hieroglyphic writings of Mayan high priests and nobles remain mostly undecipherable, it is nevertheless clear that they had a remarkably advanced understanding of mathematics, astronomy, and chronology.

Mexico's present-day capital, Mexico City, was built upon the ruins of the great Aztec capital of Tenochtitlán, founded circa 1176. Before its capture by Hernándo Cortés in 1521, Tenochtitlán was the center of a decidedly warlike and fanatically religious culture. The Aztecs were superb artisans, but the steps of their massive and lavishly decorated temples also ran with rivers of blood, as human sacrifices by the thousands were offered to the Aztecs' bloodthirsty gods during elaborate religious rituals. The divine was present in nearly every aspect of Aztec culture, and their gods demanded frequent and often violent appeasement.

According to legend, it was through just such omnipresent divinity that what would eventually become tequila was discovered: in the form of a lightning strike in a Mexican agave field. The bolt hit the heart of one of the plants, and the ensuing heat not only cooked the succulent but also caused natural fermentation to occur, producing an aromatic and intoxicating nectar.

While this tale is certainly engaging, it is only one of many legends that still swirl around the roots of tequila, originally derived as a distillate of *pulque*, a mildly alcoholic beverage produced from the indigenous agave plant, also known as *maguey* and *mezcal* in Mexico. Pulque was central to the religious ceremonies of native Mexican Indians long before the Spanish arrived. The conquistadors used their relatively new distillation techniques to create a stronger version of pulque, which they called *vino mezcal* (known variously as mezcal brandy and agave wine), as early as the mid-1520s. From there, it was only a few short steps to tequila.

Gold tequila
Yellow chartreuse

Layer 2 parts gold tequila and 1 part yellow chartreuse.

THE CHARTREUSE IN THIS SHOT will take some of the edge off almost any tequila's bite, but if you're in the mood for a smoother ride to begin with, look for "100 Percent Blue Agave" on the label of the tequila bottle (only 51 percent is required by law; most tequilas contain sugarcane distillates or have some neutral spirits added during production). One brand you might look for is Tequila Herradura, founded in 1861; an "upstart" distiller and sole challenger to the Cuervo and Sauza empires. Herradura owner-operator Guillermo Romo de la Peña is one of the few tequila makers who uses only 100 percent blue agaves in his premium estate-bottled tequilas, which contain no additives or artificial coloring. Herradura also makes a *muy anejo* tequila, four years in the wood, which is the most expensive tequila in the world—a must for connoisseurs.

Tequila

Tequila
Lime wedge
Salt

 AS THIS ALCOHOLIC RENDERING OF THE OLD CHILDREN'S RHYME SUGGESTS, tequila is sometimes imbibed in successive shots, the zealous overindulgence of which often results in a premature and infelicitous meeting with the floor. Yet available as well are quite smooth "sipping" tequilas—belying the popular misconception that all tequilas are not only alike but also spring from the same well of raw "cactus juice." Some of the finer tequilas may even be compared to fine French cognacs. But if you're determined to shoot your tequila, the classic, most commonly employed method is also still among the most fun (especially in some of its bawdier variations); that is, the "lick, sip, and suck," or salt-tequila-lime method: In your non-drinking hand, on the webbing 'twixt thumb and forefinger, sprinkle a little salt. With a shot of tequila and slice or wedge of lime already prepared, lick the salt, down the shot, then suck on the lime. *Tequila!*

The Pulqueria

Know ye what pulque is?
Liquor divine!
Angels in heaven
Prefer it to wine.

—from *Saloons of the Old West*

CALLED "THE NECTAR OF THE GODS" by Hernando Cortés, conqueror of the Aztecs, *mezcal* is derived from the Náhuatlan *mexcalmetl*, roughly meaning "species of agave" in the Uto-Aztecan language of central and southern Mexico. The word *agave* is derived from the Latin for "aristocratic." The liquor itself could be quite rough, however, and often required additional flavoring and sweetening to mask its crudely harsh rawness. Unlike tequila, which can be produced only from the blue agave, specifically from the Jalisco region (which includes the states of Guanajuato, Jalisco, Michoacán, Nayarit, and Tamaulipas), mezcal can be made anywhere in Mexico from any of several species of agave. *Mezcal de Gusanitos* includes a moth larva (often called "the worm") in the bottle, the *gusano*, which is supposed to give strength to anyone brave enough to swallow it whole.

Exported north, by the 1700s, mezcal, along with its mildly fermented, thick and milky, and much less alcoholic cousin, *pulque*, had caught on quickly in the frontier towns of the early American Southwest.

It became so popular that many saloons in that region were aptly called "pulquerias." The fact that mezcal caught on at all reflects the rough-and-tumble nature of its clientele. Described as the kind of stuff "that couldn't be corked," it could be kept only in a glass or jar and "had to be sweetened with salt before swallowing," a tradition still religiously observed to this day. Beware of angering those Aztec gods, however—too much mezcal wine was rumored to bring visions of "snakes and alligators" to the unwary drinker.

In 1795, the Spanish government granted José Maria Cuervo exclusive rights to set up the first commercial distillery of mezcal wine in the New Spain town of Tequila, which had been founded in 1656. By the mid- to later 1800s Don Cenobio Sauza had become a major competitor; it is said that Sauza determined that the blue agave was the best plant for making the type of mezcal that came to be known as tequila. Today the Cuervo and Sauza companies remain the modern tequila market leaders.

There are variations in tequila: check the labels for the basics before buying: *plata*, or silver (also called *blanco*, or white) tequila can be bottled soon after distillation, its peppery freshness sometimes accompanied by a raw, stinging bite; gold (a.k.a. *joven abocado*) tequila can be aged in oak barrels for up

At the Great Pyramid in Cholula, Puebla, is a mural, "Pulque Drinkers" that dates back to about AD 1000.

to a year, but aging is not required by Mexican law unless it's a *reposado* gold, which must be at least two months old before bottling; *añejo* tequilas are the smoothest of all and must be aged at least a year, though they often spend up to four years in the wood.

Divine Nature

In the temple by the water-reeds the god aids those who call him,
he gives them to drink.

—Hymn to Texcatzoncatl, Aztec god of pulque; translation by Daniel G. Brinton

 AMONG THE AZTEC DEITIES was a group called *Centzon Totochin* or 400 Rabbits. Their parents were Patecatl, a god of healing and fertility, and Mayahuel, who discovered pulque. The 400 represented all the forms of intoxication, and was known for holding rowdy gatherings. Try any of the following shots to create your own divine event.

Armadillo Tracks

White tequila
Rye whiskey

Shake equal parts with ice.

ARMADILLOS COME OUT AT NIGHT, because their eyes are sensitive to light—and you may find yourself avoiding daylight after a couple of these shots.

Chihuahua Sunrise

White tequila
Triple sec
Orange juice

Shake 2 parts white tequila and 1 part each triple sec and orange juice well with ice.

AZTEC LEGEND tells that the chihuahua had the power to lead the dead through the underworld. This shot might help you to emerge from that terrible underworld known as "the morning after."

Bronco Breath

Tequila
Southern Comfort

Shake equal parts well with ice.

WILL YOUR BREATH TAME A WILD HORSE after you down this indelicate little shooter? Try it and find out. To improve your exhalations, substitute white crème de menthe for the Southern Comfort.

Cancun Sunset

ON THE CUSP OF THE GULF OF MEXICO AND CARIBBEAN SEA,
Cancún lies at the northeastern tip of the Yucatán peninsula, and is home
to the Mayan ruins of Chichén Itzá, a spectacular spot from which to
view, or sip, a Cancun Sunset.

White tequila
Rose's lime juice
Grenadine

Shake 2 parts white tequila with a splash each Rose's lime juice and grenadine
well with ice.

 DURING THE HEIGHT OF MAYAN CIVILIZATION, only aristo-
crats, warriors, and priests (with exceptions made for the infirm
or aged) were allowed to drink the gift of the gods year 'round—
the regular people had to wait for the five-day festival known as
"The Days of the Dead" for their ration of pulque. Another exception was made
for prisoners of war, who were given copious quantities of pulque in preparation for
becoming sacrificial offerings to the gods. This shooter is perfect preparation for
watching the nightly sacrifice of the sun over the horizon.

Rumple Minze Peppermint Schnapps
Gold tequila

Layer equally the schnapps and gold tequila.

 THE INCAS, who considered gold to be the sweat of the gods, used it to line the walls of their magnificent Temple of the Sun in the fourteenth century. Later, the famed Aztec gold brought Cortés to defeat Montezuma and seize the Aztec gold stores for Spain. Unlike the Aztec warriors, you may not sample your tequila from a solid gold cup, but you can enjoy the same warmth with this golden shot. The mellower gold tequilas (*reposado* or *anejo*) will take the bite out of this shot. The *reposado* is smoother than *blanco* but still has the agave flavor. *Anejo* is darker in color, and its taste owes more to the wood in which it is aged than the plant from which it is derived.

Raging Bull

Kahlúa
Sambuca
Gold tequila

Layer equally.

OUTSIDE OF THE BULLFIGHTING RING, you're more likely to come in contact with sufferers of raging hormones more often than victims of stampeding bulls, but either one may require immediate attention—medical or, um, otherwise. With little training, almost anyone can become a tequila body-shot EMT, breathing new life into the old "lick, sip, and suck" method. You'll need a partner willing to bare some skin—and to be licked. No hands are required at all to hit this bull's-eye: place a shot of tequila and a pinch of salt on the lickee's skin (the belly, between the breasts, and the hollow of the neck are all possible locations, or be creative and think of your own). Place a lime wedge, pulp out, in your partner's mouth; then lick the salt, tip the shot back (remember, no hands), and suck on that lime.

Bull Shots

BULLFIGHTING IS A TRADITION IMPORTED FROM SPAIN that has been popular in Mexico since its first bullfight took place in Mexico City in 1526 to honor Cortés. These shots may excite your own inner bull.

Brave Bull

White tequila
Kahlúa

Layer equally or shake Kahlúa and white tequila with ice.

Bull by the Horns

White tequila
Vodka
Light rum

Shake equal parts with ice.

White Bull

White tequila
Kahlúa
Cream or half-and-half

Pour equal parts tequila and Kahlúa. Add cream or half-and-half to taste and shake really well.

Bullseye

Tequila
Tabasco sauce

Add a couple drops of Tabasco sauce to your tequila shot, and here's mud in your eye!

Electric Banana

IT'S ELECTRIC! Boogie woogie, woogie!

—Marcia Griffiths, "Electric Boogie"

White tequila
Crème de banane
Rose's lime juice

Shake 2 parts white tequila with 1 part each crème de banane and Rose's lime juice well with ice.

 ONCE YOU'VE MASTERED THE ELECTRIC BANANA, why not try the Electric Slide? Whether a budding line-dance or stand-up career emerges from your initial attempt will depend on how many shots go down first. Here are some *simple* instructions for you!

1. Step to the right with right foot

2. Slide left foot right and hook behind right foot

3. Step to the right again with right foot (unhook left first)

4. Slide left foot beside right foot and clap

5. Repeat steps 1 through 4 while slide-stepping to the left

Hop, Skip, & Run Naked, see page 87

Rumrunners, Inc.

There's nought, no doubt, so much the spirit calms as rum and true religion.

—Lord Byron, *Don Juan*

IN THE WAKE OF COLUMBUS'S FATEFUL VOYAGE to the New World came the discovery of sugarcane (*Saccharum officinarum*) in the West Indies. This previously rare but now suddenly cheap and abundant commodity was immediately capitalized upon by early Spanish colonizers, who in a relatively short period of time experimented with the distillation of molasses, a product of sugarcane. ("Molasses" is the English translation of what the Spanish called *melazas*, itself an adaptation of *miel*, Spanish for honey.) The resulting witches' brew, best known as "rumbowling" among sailors, was first called "rumbullion" or "rumbustion."

The "Barbados Brandy" appears in the historical record by the mid-1600s, when the fiery beverage was also known as Kill-Devil, Devil's Death, and Nelson's Blood and described as a "hot, hellish, and terrible liquor." First imported to the American colonies as early as 1640, rumbullion was well on its way to becoming essential to the fledgling economy by the time it came to be called simply rum, about 1667.

Not long after its first appearance there the colonies were awash in a "sea of rum," with the infamous triangular rum trade well established circa 1700. For at least the next 70 years, native West Africans were taken as slaves to the West Indies, where they were traded for molasses and forced to labor in the sugarcane fields; the molasses was then shipped to New England for distillation into rum; the rum in turn was exported back to Africa in return for more slaves.

The colonists of the New World weren't alone in their ardent appreciation of the tropical spirit, however, and rum (in the form of a watered-down naval "grog") became "indispensable" to the British military, as explained by General Clinton in 1781: "The severe duty and portion of fatigue that falls to the lot of troops…make rum of importance [in the colonies]." In fact, British sailors continued to receive regular rum rations—often in the form of a daily "gill," or about half a pint of rum mixed with water—until 1970. Rum was, after all, considered a virtual cure-all for everything from battle fatigue to low morale and colds and influenza to a "waning of the genitories"—colonial Viagra, anyone?

British appreciation didn't stop at consumption, however, as there were hefty profits to be "shared." To this end, in 1733 England imposed prohibitive duties on rum and the essentials of its production in a blatant attempt to force the American colonies to import sugarcane and molasses from the British West Indies exclusively. Largely unsuccessful for the English, the Molasses Act rather served to sow the seeds of rebellion, turning savvy sailors into smugglers and struggling merchants into rumrunners—and affecting future American tariff policies for many years to come.

Hop, Skip, & Run Naked

CAPTAIN SAYS... Streaking in public can get you arrested, check with local authorities before stripping down to your birthday suit and skipping gleefully across the sand as Nature may or may not have intended.

Captain Morgan's Spiced Rum
Vodka
Apricot brandy
Grenadine
Rose's lime juice

Pour 1 part Captain Morgan's and 1 part vodka, then add a splash each of apricot brandy, grenadine, and lime juice. Shake very well with ice.

CAPTAIN HENRY MORGAN (1635–1688) was one of the most famous buccaneers of the West Indies. Originally from Wales, he eventually settled in Jamaica, where he was a representative of the British crown. In between, he sailed on numerous expeditions to attack Spanish ships and settlements—and became quite wealthy in the process. It was said of Morgan that he liked his rum. Captain Morgan's Spiced Rum, a golden rum laced with spices, was named in his honor.

Funky Monkey

Why did the monkey cross the road? It was the chicken's day off.

Light rum
Crème de banane
Dark crème de cacao
Half-and-half
Whipped cream

STEP 1: Shake equal amounts of rum, crème de banane, crème de cacao, and half-and-half well with ice.

STEP 2: Pour into glasses.

STEP 3: Top off with whipped cream.

THIS CREAMY AND STICKY SHOT IS ALSO KNOWN AS SEX ON THE LAKE. If you'd prefer Sex with the Captain on the Lake, never mind the crème and creams, use spiced rum instead of light, and add peach schnapps plus a healthy splash of pineapple juice. It will still be sweet and sticky, but not creamy. Another variation, in which you can bring your Smelly Cat along for the ride, calls for switching Bacardi Limón for the spiced rum and adding cranberry juice.

RUM IS MADE WHEREVER THE CANE WILL GROW—primarily the Caribbean islands. Some 80 percent of rum consumed in the United States comes from Puerto Rico. Light rum and dark rum are the main categories, with gold, or medium, rum; spiced rum; and 151 proof rum making up the rest.

Toasted in Jamaica

Wray and Nephew's Overproof Rum
Milk

Pour equal measure each.

APPLETON ESTATE, the home of Wray & Nephew's "finest rums," dates to 1749, making it the oldest sugar estate and distillery in Jamaica.

Calypso

Myers's Original Dark Jamaican Rum
Tia Maria Coffee Liqueur

Pour equal measure each and shoot—both spirits are at their best and make for a perfect match at room temperature.

ACCORDING TO LEGEND, during the colonial wars in seventeenth-century Jamaica a Spanish noblewoman fled her home and, amidst the confusion of escape, her maid, Tia Maria, had just enough time to grab a few treasured possessions, including a family recipe for a cordial. In gratitude, the woman named the cordial after the intrepid maid.

Sunny Delight

Light rum
Orange juice
Pineapple juice
Sugar

Pour 2 parts light rum, 1 part each of the orange and pineapple juice and add a teaspoon of sugar. Shake very well with ice.

"RED SKIES AT NIGHT, sailors' delight; red skies at morning, sailors take warning"—and sunny skies all day make the sugarcane ripe.

Pez

Candy is dandy but liquor is quicker.

—Ogden Nash

Captain Morgan's Spiced Rum
Chambord Royale

Shake each well with ice.

 CHAMBORD ROYALE is an imported French cognac infused with black raspberries, to which such spices as cinnamon, cloves, ginger, and vanilla are added along with honey, orange, and lemon extracts before the whole mix returns to the wood for additional aging. Mixed with the complementary flavors of the Captain's spiced rum, it makes for a fruity but complex concoction. Think of it as candy for grown-ups...and if it leads to indulging in any other adult pleasures, well, so much the better.

Put the lime in the coconut and drink them both together.
Put the lime in the coconut and then you feel better.

—Harry Nilsson, "Coconut"

Myers's Dark Rum
Coconut water
Rose's lime juice

Pour 2 parts Myers's Dark Rum and 1 part coconut in with a splash of Rose's lime juice. Shake well with ice.

BRITISH VICE-ADMIRAL EDWARD VERNON became the father of grog in 1740 when, in an effort to quell the drunkenness and lack of discipline that came with issuing rum to sailors, he ordered that rum rations be mixed with water and suggested adding sugar and lime for taste. The rations were distributed twice a day, between 10 A.M. and 12 P.M. and between 4 and 6 P.M., by the call to "Up Spirits." In 1824, the ration was reduced from a $1/2$ pint to $2^1/2$ ounces, or a "tot." On January 28, 1970, the House of Commons held the Great Rum Debate and July 30, 1970, known as "Black Tot Day," was the last call to Up Spirits for grog.

Light rum

Jägermeister

Rumple Minze Peppermint Schnapps

Pour equal parts each and shake very well with ice.

IN NAUTICAL TERMS, "sheets," rather than being used to make the bed, are the ropes or chains attached to the lower corner of a sail that serve to shorten or extend it. Thus three-sailed vessels such as ketches typically employed three sheets. With one sheet loose, or "in the wind," as the original phrase went, a sail would flap about and throw the ketch off course. Two sheets loose meant serious trouble. And three? That ship's bound to reel about "like a drunken sailor," of course.

Sacrelicious

A cooler bat symbol than that Goody-Two-shoes from Gotham's.

Bacardi Limón
Midori
Rose's lime juice

Shake well with ice.

ACCORDING TO THE COMPANY, Bacardi's famous bat device was designed in 1862 by Doña Amalia Lucía Victorio Moreau, wife of Bacardi founder Don Facundo. While surveying their Cuban estate, Amalia saw a colony of fruit bats living in the distillery's rafters. As local beliefs held that bats brought good health, fortune, and family unity, she designed the symbol to distinguish Bacardi from other rums.

Because the sugar required for fermentation is already present in the raw material—molasses—rum tends to retain more of a "raw-material taste" than most spirits, with characteristic flavors often determined rather by the type of yeast used, the distillation method, the conditions under which it is aged and stored, and the blending of various rum batches. For those less enamored of the more traditional rum tate, Bacardi Limón, with its lower proof and citrus tang, may be the perfect remedy.

Rum Mates

BARBADOS AND TRINIDAD Light to medium rums, though smokier varieties, with a taste akin to the charred-cask overtones of some Scotches, are available.

BRITISH GUYANA Basic light and dark varieties, the light is drunk locally while the dark, known as *Demerara* and highly regarded, is exported—most of it to England. This exported variety, rich and full-bodied, is used frequently in cooking, especially in puddings, and is perfect over ice cream or in cakes and frosting.

CUBA Generally lighter and prized for their delicate, dry flavor, though darker and higher-proof rums from the island are also available.

JAMAICA Light-, medium-, and heavy-bodied rums.

MARTINIQUE Aromatic, medium-bodied rums run mostly dark from the island's patent-still majority. Excellent in black coffee or over ice cream.

PUERTO RICO Favored for their lightness—especially in the U.S., where light (white label) and lighter (gold label) still tend to vie for popularity.

Rumrunner

Light rum
Dark rum
Pineapple juice
Rose's lime juice

Pour 1 part each light rum, dark rum, and pineapple juice, plus a splash of Rose's lime juice, and shake very well with ice.

THE RUMRUNNERS OF THE 1920S AND EARLY '30S served a flourishing bootlegger's market between the U.S. and Canada in the shadow of American Prohibition, brazenly crisscrossing the Great Lakes in often armor-clad "gray ghosts"—sleek, low-lying boats designed to outrun the Coast Guard's cutters. In Detroit, where teetotalers like Henry Ford tried to impress sobriety on the common man, illegal liquor was the second-most profitable industry in 1929, after automobiles. The frozen Detroit River made winter transportation easy and the river's thousands of coves along the banks and in islands made hiding from patrols a year-round breeze. Meanwhile, rum was being sped down the California coast and driven or carried across the U.S.-Canadian border at every possible point.

Solaris

A spoonful of sugar...

Captain Morgan's Spiced Rum
Grenadine
Sugar

Pour 2 parts Captain Morgan's Spiced Rum and 1 part grenadine. Add a teaspoon of sugar and shake very well with ice.

 IMAGINE IT: sitting on an empty, gleaming white beach, staring at a coral reef through crystal clear water that reflects the golden sun in an azure sky, while a slight breeze whispers through the palm trees. That's when you reach for this sweet and spicy, enlightening shot. For those colder days on stormy seas, mix up a batch of the Captain's Toddies: pour three shots of spiced rum into a ceramic milk server. Add half a cup of boiling water,* and honey (or sugar) to taste. Yields about 8 shots.

*These little hot shots should cool down enough by the time they're mixed and poured, but please check them anyway before you go knocking 'em straight back.

Candy Cane, see page 104

Seasonal Shooters and Dessert Drams

I drink when I have occasion, and sometimes when I have no occasion.

—Miguel de Cervantes, *Don Quixote*

I COULD NOT AGREE MORE. When it comes to seasonal shooters, there are just a few guidlines. It's often better to keep it light in warmer weather—especially if you plan to do your toasting outdoors. Just about anything shaken with ice and fruit juice to lower the alcohol content can make for a breezy summertime cooler. Save the heavier cordials, harder straight-up shots, and creamier dessert shooters for the winter holidays, a time of year traditionally rife with ritual as well as the best season for liqueurs.

Whatever your occasion, be it a casual after-dinner toast, a festive summer picnic, or a blowout holiday bash, you're sure to find among the following little big drinks just the one to toast the moment.

Candy Is Dandy

READY for a little something sweet?

CORDIALS ARE THE PERFECT DESSERT DRINKS. Sweetened with the addition of herbs, berries, and flowers, they often have a pleasing aroma as well as taste. These sweet elixirs are better sipped than downed in one shot. And if your sweetie feels sweeter than usual after drinking one of these, well, don't say I didn't warn you.

Candy Cane

Grenadine
Vodka
Green crème de menthe

Layer equally in a tallish shot glass grenadine, vodka, and green crème de menthe.

Bonbon

Rumple Minze Peppermint Schnapps
Godiva Chocolate Liqueur

Shake equal parts Rumple Minze and Godiva very well with ice and strain.

Jelly Bean

Anisette
Blackberry brandy

Layer equally the anisette and brandy.

EVEN IF YOU DON'T LIKE JELLY BEANS, you have to appreciate a shot that gives the adults something to do while the kids are (hopefully) entirely engaged in an annual Easter Egg Hunt. Originally named for Eostre, the Saxon goddess of spring whose festival was held at the equinox, Easter was adopted by the Christian Church to commemorate Jesus' resurrection. Decorated eggs were initially given as gifts to symbolize rebirth and renewal at spring's arrival.

Grey's Peppermints

Grey Goose Vodka
Peppermint schnapps

Shake equal parts ice-cold Grey Goose and schnapps well with ice, then strain for one wickedly minty wallop of a shot.

DISTILLED AND BOTTLED IN COGNAC, FRANCE, the award-winning Grey Goose claims to be the "most requested ultra-premium vodka in the United States" and is the "best-tasting vodka in the world," according to the Beverage Testing Institute.

After Eight

There's a good time coming, boys!

—Charles Mackay, "The Good Time Coming"

Kahlúa
Bailey's Irish Cream
White crème de menthe

Shake equal parts Kahlúa, Bailey's, and white crème de menthe very well with ice and strain into shot glasses.

WHO CARES WHETHER ANYBODY REALLY KNOWS WHAT TIME IT IS? It's all relative—making anytime a good time to celebrate the evening. This dessert shot tastes a lot like those after-dinner chocolate-covered mint candies that appear on hotel room pillows. The mint-chocolate combination is a classic—two tastes that were made for each other. In fact, chocolate was created by the Maya from local cacao beans, as early as AD 500. Mint, native to Europe and western Asia has an even longer history, dating back at least to ancient Greece. So enjoy this shot, knowing that time is on your side.

Apple Pie

SERVE Á LA MODE or on its own.

Vodka
Applejack Apple Brandy
Apple juice
Cinnamon

STEP 1: Shake 2 parts vodka, 1 part Applejack, and a healthy splash of apple juice well with ice.

STEP 2: Strain into shot glasses, topping each off with a pinch of cinnamon for that homey touch.

NOTHING SAYS "COMFORT" SO WELL AS a slice of apple pie. Applejack is a blend of apple brandy and neutral spirits. First bottled in the 1600s, apple brandy was (and is) made from pure apple juice. One bottle of Applejack contains approximately 6 pounds of apples! And you know what they say about an apple a day...

Baby Grasshopper

SCIENTIFICALLY, a baby grasshopper is called a nymph.

Green crème de menthe
White crème de cacao
Cream
Whipped cream (optional)

STEP 1: Shake equal parts crème de menthe and crème de cacao plus a splash of cream very well with ice.

STEP 2: Strain into shot glasses for miniature versions of this sweet and classic after-dinner cocktail.

STEP 3: Top with whipped cream.

MINTY, CHOCOLATY, AND CREAMY, this dessert shot will have you hopping. For a south-of-the-border twist, replace the crème de cacao with Kahlúa and call it a Mexican Grasshopper. For a Flying Grasshopper, replace the cream with vodka and add a cherry garnish. If you want a dessert to match, you can make a grasshopper pie—the filling comprises the ingredients above, and the crust (or shell) is graham crackers.

Banana Split

WARNING: Do not attempt gymnastics while drinking these.

Crème de banane
Crème de almond
Kahlúa
Whipped cream
Maraschino cherry

STEP 1: Shake equal parts crème de banane and crème de almond plus a splash of Kahlúa very well with ice and strain.

STEP 2: Top off with whipped cream and a maraschino cherry to add the crowning touch to this nutty little dessert shooter—and its tropical sensibility makes it perfect for summertime gatherings.

BANANA TRIVIA

1) Bananas originated in Malaysia. Alexander the Great is credited with bringing them to the West after his campaign in India in 327 BC.

2) Banana trees are not trees. They are giant herbaceous plants. But bananas themselves are fruit, not herbs.

3) The banana split was invented in 1904 in Strickler's Drug Store in Latrobe, Pennsylvania.

Black Widow

This is Halloween, everybody make a scene.
Trick or treat till the neighbors gonna die of fright.

—Danny Elfman, "This Is Halloween"

Black sambuca
White sambuca
Grenadine

Layer black and white sambuca equally, then top it off with a drop of grenadine in the center of the shot glass.

THIS SCARY LITTLE SHOOTER IS A NATURAL COME HALLOWEEN—traditionally a night when witches and goblins are believed to walk the earth. On October 31, eve of the Celtic new year (known as "Hallowmas" or "All Saint's Day"), the festival of *Samhain*, or "Old Year's Night," was celebrated to welcome the spirits of the dead. The ancient Celts believed that on *Samhain* the barriers between the human and spirit worlds were weak enough to allow the souls of the dead into our world to search for light and heat. The living lit bonfires to welcome the wandering spirits, while keeping mischievous ones away.

Champagne
Chambord Royale

Pour 2 parts champagne to 1 part (or to taste) Chambord Royale straight up.

FOR THOSE OF YOU WHO DON'T LIKE THE DRYNESS OF MANY CHAMPAGNES, this is the perfect addition to an auld New Year's Eve tradition—whether you prefer a shot or a cocktail, your evening just got a little sweeter….

In 1856, Moët & Chandon, makers of Dom Perignon, first produced wine with a lower sugar dosage, earning it the category of "dry" on the label. These new dry champagnes were made for the British market when it was discovered that they were drinking iced champagne.

Brain Hemorrhage

I can feel my mind going....

—Arthur C. Clarke, *2001: A Space Odyssey*

Peach schnapps
Grenadine
Bailey's Irish Cream

STEP 1: Fill a shot glass ²/₃ full with schnapps.

STEP 2: Carefully layer last third with Bailey's.

STEP 3: Add a drop of grenadine. Eeeuuw, gross...another great Halloween shot!

 REMEMBER THOSE COMMERCIALS with the voice-over, "This is your brain...this is your brain on drugs," during which the camera pans in with an overhead shot of two sunny-side up eggs in a big iron skillet loudly frying away in at least an inch of oil? At least that's the version I remember best—it made me hungry. Had the Partnership for a Drug-Free America simply employed a close-up of a Brain Hemorrhage instead, the point would have had far greater impact.

Butterball

Butterscotch schnapps
Brandy

Layer equally butterscotch schnapps and brandy.

BRANDY HAS ALWAYS BEEN PART OF AMERICA: When Henry Hudson sailed into New York Harbor aboard the *Half Moon* in 1609, he brought along a generous supply of brandy—the sustaining eau-de-vie was considered indispensable during long months at sea.

And most Americans know all about the first Thanksgiving, but a story not as oft told concerns part of the reason (or legend) the *Mayflower* made it only as far as Plymouth Rock in Massachusetts on its way to Virginia—brandy from wine was being distilled right on board during the arduous voyage, but the poor pilgrims were nearly out of "beere" by the time they had crossed the Atlantic.

Chocolate Nut Poundcake

HAZELNUT AND LEMON give this shot a sweet-tart bite.

Absolut Citron
Frangelico Hazelnut Liqueur
Sugar
Lemon wedge or half-wheel

STEP 1: Shake Citron and Frangelico well with ice.

STEP 2: Strain, knock back, then suck on an already-prepared sugarcoated lemon wedge or half-wheel.

THERE'S NO NEED FOR BAKED GOODS when Frangelico's in the house (though it is a popular liqueur for cooking). With a subtle bouquet of hazelnuts and butter topped off with hints of berries and flowers from a secret recipe, this lovely liqueur also fares well all on its own. Developed in the seventeenth century at a monastery in the hilly Piedmont region of Italy, Frangelico bears the name of the hermit-monk who created the recipe.

Chiquita

Time flies like an arrow; fruit flies like a banana.

—Groucho Marx

Vodka

Crème de banane

Milk

Blend 3 parts vodka, 2 parts crème de banane, and 12 parts milk with about 1/2 cup of ice.

MEDICINAL QUALITITES OF BANANAS:

Stress	Potassium regulates the heartrate.
Heartburn	Bananas are natural antacids.
Strokes	The New England Journal of Medicine says eating bananas regularly may reduce the risk of death from stroke.
Ulcers	Soft texture and smoothness coats the stomach lining.
Nerves	B vitamins calm the nervous system.
Hangover	In a milkshake, the banana calms the stomach and rebuilds sugar levels while the milk soothes and rehydrates.

Jelly Donut

To alcohol! The cause of, and solution to, all of life's problems.

—Homer J. Simpson

Black raspberry schnapps
Half-and-half
Powdered confectioner's sugar

STEP 1: Shake 2 parts schnapps and 1 part half-and-half very well with ice.

STEP 2: Strain and top off with a pinch of powdered confectioners' sugar.

 "MMM...DONUTS." Homer Simpson, king of gluttony and sloth, said a mouthful there. But what does that other, slightly less-well-known Homer have to say about food, drink, and rest? "Now, therefore, let us all do as I say; we have eaten and drunk our fill, let us then take our rest, for in rest there is both strength and stay." — *The Iliad*; translation by Samuel Butler

Irish Flag

EVERYONE'S EYES will be smiling.

Green crème de menthe
Bailey's Irish Cream
Brandy

Layer equally green crème de menthe, Bailey's, and brandy to represent the three equal bands of the Irish "Tricolor."

IRELAND'S NATIONAL FLAG WAS FIRST UNFURLED IN 1848, its colors reflecting the Irish political landscape of the time, according to writer Burgna Brunner. Orange became the patriotic color for Irish Protestants of the north because of King William III of Orange, who defeated the Catholic Jacobites in 1690. Green is the color of Irish Catholics from the south. The band of white in the center symbolizes hope for peace between the Irish Protestants and their Catholic kinsmen.

This is a perfect shot to serve during annual St. Patrick's Day celebrations, which honor Ireland's patron saint. An official bank holiday in the north, March 17 is a day to commemorate the life and work of Saint Patrick (approximately AD 389–461), a key figure in bringing Christianity to Ireland. Born in Great Britain, he was enslaved by pirates for six years before escaping and devoting the rest of his life to missionary work. A unifying Irish tradition involves the wearing of the clover-like shamrock, a cherished national symbol of both north and south.

Jell-O Sunset

For art to exist, for any sort of aesthetic activity to exist, a certain physiological precondition is indispensable: intoxication.

—Friedrich Nietzsche, *Twilight of the Idols*

Lemon Jell-O
Black Cherry Jell-O
Water
Alcohol

STEP 1: Using clear plastic shot glasses (available at larger liquor stores and/or party supply stores) or small salsa containers (available with lids from party and/or restaurant supply stores), make a batch of lemon Jell-O (add Jell-O to one cup of boiling water and allow to cool before adding one cup vodka; stir well). Fill shot glasses halfway and refrigerate until firm (usually about three hours or so).

STEP 2: Make a second batch of black cherry Jell-O but do not refrigerate. Allow it to cool (so as not to melt the bottom layer) just enough to pour, then slowly top off the shots with the black cherry Jell-O. Now sit back and enjoy the show! (Yields 12 shots.)

JELL-O, born 1897. Nietzsche, died 1900. Coincidence?

Jellyfish

YOU'LL BE SHOCKED when it gets its tentacles around you.

White crème de cacao
Amaretto
Bailey's Irish Cream
Grenadine

STEP 1: Shake equal parts white crème de cacao and amaretto well with ice.

STEP 2: Strain into a shot glass or glasses, leaving room to float about a third of Bailey's on top.

STEP 3: Add a dash of grenadine.

 ANYONE WHO'S SPENT TIME NEAR THE OCEAN knows that after a storm there will be a number of jellyfish washed up on the beach. Walking along the beach in the just-cooled summer air is an experience everyone should have at least once. This shot reminds me of walks like those. The effort required to produce the desired tentacled effect of this shot is well worth it—and perfect for kicking off the summer season on Memorial Day or for closing it out on Labor Day.

Nickler

THERE'S A LOT TO THINK ABOUT, but you'll be thankful.

Brandy
Lemon wheel
Sugar
Instant or finely ground coffee

STEP 1: Pour a tall shot of brandy.

STEP 2: Thinly slice a lemon wheel and pour sugar on one half and coffee on the other.

STEP 3: Serve the shot with the coffee- and sugar-coated lemon slice on top.

STEP 4: The designated drinker should then carefully fold the lemon wheel in half and bite it off at the rind just before knocking back the brandy— just remember to chew and swallow the lemon, etc., first.

 ACCORDING TO ONE LEGEND, coffee was discovered by an Ethiopian goatherd named Kaldi who noticed that his goats were more energetic after eating the red berries of a local shrub. He decided to try the berries himself and soon found that he felt a little wired, too. He then shared the fruit with a wandering imam, who dried and boiled it.

Peppermint Paddy

EVER GET THE SENSATION that your taste buds will never be quite the same again? Or the feeling that the floor is probably a lot more comfortable than it looks? No? Then you haven't tried a Peppermint Paddy.

Peppermint schnapps
Kahlúa
Bailey's Irish Cream

Layer in equal parts.

 JUST ABOUT EVERYBODY at some point in their early drinking days becomes familiar with peach or peppermint schnapps—even if not your personal choice, chances are you knew somebody who knew someone who liked the stuff.

The majority of flavored schnapps makes for smoother shooting best for the palate unaccustomed to harder alcohol's bite. At a usually lower proof, peppermint schnapps goes down easy, and the better brands (more natural mint, less flavored sugar) will freshen your breath in the bargain. Schnapps as we know it has come a long way from its German and Dutch origins, however, where *Schnaps* was another name for "spirit" and was distilled primarily from potatoes. Similar to the Scandinavian aquavit (also produced from potatoes and sometimes grain, and often flavored with aromatic herbs and spices), schnapps is best served chilled and neat, and is usually swigged rather than sipped.

St. Valentine's Day Massacre

YOU'LL FEEL untouchable.

Tequila
Chambord Royale

Just pour tequila and Chambord in equal parts (or 2-to-1 in favor of the tequila) straight up.

 DURING THE HEIGHT OF PROHIBITION, mob gangs made Chicago a dangerous playground, rife with guns, gambling, and bootlegging. A fierce rivalry between Al Capone and "Bugs" Moran led to the infamous St. Valentine's Day Massacre, in which seven gangsters were lined up and shot. Capone was rumored to be behind it, but was never charged. For a gentler sort of Valentine's Day celebration, try one of these — and make love, not war.

Sweet Old Glory

Hail the red, white, and blue.

Grenadine
White crème de cacao
Blue curaçao

Layer grenadine, crème de cacao, and blue curaçao equally in a tallish (but narrow) shot glass.

 IF YOU'RE LOOKING FOR FIREWORKS, KEEP LOOKING. Not only is the alcohol content extremely low here—not necessarily a bad thing at all, especially for a summertime shot—but the emphasis is definitely on *sweet*. And thick. More than one is more than enough. It is mighty pretty, though. Think of it as a onetime party favor kind of thing, a door prize on the Fourth of July, perhaps. Don't forget to raise your glass to Francis Scott Key, who adapted a popular British drinking song called "To Anacreon" into "The Star-Spangled Banner." (Anacreon, by the way, was an ancient Greek poet known for his odes in praise of wine and women.)

Sambuca, see page 139

Last Call

Closing time—one last call for alcohol, so finish your whiskey or beer.
Closing time—you don't have to go home, but you can't stay here.

—Semisonic, "Closing Time"

IT ARRIVES AS EARLY AS 10:20 P.M. IN LONDON, at which point the bell really does toll for thee as the publican declares, "Last orders, ladies and gentlemen!"—signaling only forty minutes before closing time (midnight to 1 A.M. on weekends). In Amsterdam, Anchorage, Chicago, and Toronto the night stretches out still later, as most bars stay open 'til three. If you can't even imagine going home before four, you'll be in good company whenever you're in New York City or Puerto Rico, and you won't have to leave the *Kneipe* before six in Munich, while in Berlin most bars are open simply "late." Acapulco and New Orleans impose no closing time whatsoever. Nearly wherever you are, the tradition of the last call is an old and venerable one. At its merriest it's a time to raise a toast to good times, good health, good friends, and to wish one and all the very best... Cheers!

Travel Tipples

EXPLORE NEW CULTURES...without ever leaving home.

ALMOST EVERY CULTURE AND REGION in the world has its own drinking traditions and unique tipples. Sampling them is one of the great pleasures of travel. But if you're more of an armchair traveler, you can still enjoy a multicultural drinking experience with these shots that hail from various places around the world.

Aloha

Kona Gold Coffee Liqueur
Amaretto
Coconut milk

Shake equal parts Kona Gold and Amaretto plus a splash of coconut milk very well with ice.

WHETHER YOU'RE COMING OR GOING ON THE BIG ISLAND, *aloha* is more than a simple greeting or salutation, and holds a much deeper meaning for the Hawaiian people: "To hear what is not said, to see what cannot be seen, and to know the unknowable."

Boswandeling

Vodka
Triple sec
Angostura Aromatic Bitters

Shake 2 parts vodka, 1 part triple sec, and 5 dashes Angostura very well with ice.

DESCRIBED AS ORIGINATING FROM "one of the oldest bars in Amsterdam," *boswandeling* roughly translates as "a walk in the woods"—something you definitely *do not* want to go for after one too many of these Kamikazi-like shooters.

Sambuca

Sambuca
Coffee beans

Pour the sambuca; float three beans on top.

ALSO THE NAME OF AN ANCIENT GREEK HARP, possibly Syrian or Phoenician in origin, sambuca is a not-too-sweet, anise-flavored Italian liqueur, traditionally served with two or three roasted coffee beans floating on top. Otherwise clear and colorless, this popular after-dinner liqueur turns cloudy when mixed with water or served on the rocks.

Antifreeze

Vodka

Melon liqueur

Shake equal parts vodka and melon well with ice and strain.

 WHEN YOU NEED A LITTLE EXTRA PROTECTION FROM THE ELEMENTS—or just want to take your buzz on the road— this is the shot for you. (Along with this piece of advice from Dean Martin, "If you drink, don't drive. Don't even putt.")

As good as all our manufactured concoctions are, chemists are still trying to figure out how antifreeze proteins in fish like flounder and cod prevent them from icing up in below-freezing temperatures. They've studied eveything from hydrogen bonding to interactions of the protein's structure with ice to hydrophobic interaction, but so far, no dice. Silly scientists—the fish must be drinking shots.

Coffee Time

HOW DO YOU take your coffee?

THE COMBINATION OF COFFEE AND ALCOHOL is a happy one, with the caffeine sharpening the exhilaration of the booze at first, then combating the depressive effects. Try any of these coffee-based shooters for a pick-me-up.

Al Cappuccino

Tiramisu Italian coffee liqueur
Amaretto
Whipped cream
Cinnamon

STEP 1: Shake equal parts tiramisu and amaretto very well with ice.

STEP 2: Strain into shot glasses, leaving enough room to top each off with a small dollop of whipped cream.

STEP 3: Sprinkle with cinnamon.

B-50s

B51: Bailey's Irish Cream, Kahlúa, and Frangelico

B52: Kahlúa, Grand Marnier, and Bailey's

B53: Kahlúa, vodka, and Bailey's

B54: Kahlúa, tequila, and Bailey's

YOU COULD TRY TO EQUALLY LAYER THESE SHOOTERS, but just shaking them up with ice will make your life much easier—perhaps something to keep in mind next time you're out. For example, asking your bartender to layer *any* shot during a busy last call probably won't win you any favors (though that kind of behavior is admittedly preferable to tossing beer coasters in his general direction in a drunken play for attention).

T.K.O.

Tequila
Kahlúa
Ouzo

Pour equal parts tequila, Kahlúa, and ouzo straight up into a shot glass—don't worry about layering, as that'll be the least of your problems after one too many of these. This shot's name *is* accurate.

Baby Guinness

Erin go bragh, baby.

Kahlúa

Bailey's Irish Cream

Layer in a shot glass at least 2 parts Kahlúa to 1 part Bailey's (which serves as the collar of foam for this "beer").

 DON'T HAVE THE TIME or stomach for a full pint, then? Just scale it down a notch. If you can find a mini beer mug, even better, as this shot works best when most resembling a wee pint. Just remember, if you send it back because the head's too thick, the bartender may get quite angry. It may not smell like Guinness and it may not taste like Guinness, but it looks like Guinness and you won't be complaining when the combination of coffee and cream liqueurs slides down your throat as easily as the stout.

Get Schnappered

SOMETIMES A LITTLE SHOT is all you need.

 GETTING "SCHNAPPERED" may not always be a bad thing. A man in Germany was caught in an avalanche and was buried unconscious for two hours before he could be found. When he was dug out, he was revived with a shot of... you guessed it. While these shots may not wake you up, you'll definitely feel warmer after drinking one.

Bad Habit

Vodka
Peach schnapps

Layer equally (or shake well with ice, your call) vodka and peach schnapps.

Terminator

Jack Daniel's Tennessee Whiskey
Peppermint schnapps

Shake equal parts Jack Daniel's and peppermint schnapps well with ice.

Rocky Road to Ruin

FASTEN your seatbelts.

Bailey's Irish Cream
Irish Mist
Wild Turkey 101

STEP 1: Shake equal parts Bailey's and Irish Mist well with ice.

STEP 2: Strain about $2/3$ into shot glasses, leaving room to float Wild Turkey 101 on top.

THE TRADITIONAL IRISH WAKE—an occasion of equally mixed celebration and sadness—became a somewhat different sort of affair in the mid-1800s, when waves of Irish immigrants landed on American shores. Before leaving Ireland, the hopeful emigrant would be thrown a final party, often the last chance to spend time with friends and family soon to be left behind.

REMEMBER those lunchtime snacks in a tin can? Peaches, grapes, pineapple, pears, and red cherries cut into small slices and drowned in heavy syrup. These shots taste nothing like that, but are quite tasty anyway. Maybe if you did each one in succession, you could recreate the experience a little bit, without cutting your tongue on the metal rim of the can as you try to get every bit of liquid out. Or was I the only one who did that?

Lemon Drop

Vodka
Lemon Juice
Sugar

STEP 1: Shake 2 parts vodka, 1 part lemon juice, and sugar to taste very well with ice.

STEP 2: Strain.

THE FIRST TIME I HAD A LEMON DROP was at the Rover's pub in San Francisco. I practically melted into the cab for the ride back home. That's how I remember it, at least.

Waltzing Matilda

Dark rum
Blue curaçao
Pineapple juice

Care for a last dance? Shake a shot of dark rum with a splash each of blue curaçao and pineapple juice well with ice and strain.

IN THE LAND DOWN UNDER, the phrase "waltzing Matilda" came to mean traveling from place to place in search of work with all your belongings wrapped in a blanket and strapped to your back.

Waterloo

Mandarin Napoléon Liqueur
Light rum
Orange juice

Shake equal parts Mandarin Napoléon Liqueur and light rum plus a splash of orange juice well with ice and strain.

BEFORE YOU FINALLY RAISE THAT WHITE FLAG, it seems only fitting to leave you with a song: "One for My Baby (And One More for the Road)."

Banzai Pipeline

IT'S NOT JUST for surfers anymore.

Wild Turkey 101
Midori
Bacardi 151

Layer in a shot glass 2 parts Wild Turkey and Midori, then top off with a splash of Bacardi for the last third.

 IN JAPAN, where the after-work cocktail is viewed as an important way to unwind from a stressful business day, one of the standard toasts is *banzai*, meaning "May you live a thousand years." However, you really are taking a chance with that toast's influence if you try to surf the Banzai Pipeline at Oahu's Ehukai Beach. During the rough winter surf, waves can reach over twenty-five feet (7.5 meters) before breaking hard on a shallow reef. Like the shot, this surf's not for amateurs.

I'm gonna get ya, get ya, get ya.

—Blondie, "One Way or Another"

AH, ROMANCE.... From our earliest, nervous encounters to beautiful one-night-stands with strangers while on vacation to the truly mature decision to spend the rest of your life with someone because you can feel the cold barrel of a rifle digging into your spine. Ok, most people's love lives aren't that eventful, but there's no reason you can't live vicariously through your drink names. Just remember, when you hear that click, it really is time to settle down or get out of Dodge.

Busted Cherry

Tia Maria
Cherry brandy
Cream

Shake equal parts Tia Maria, cherry brandy, and cream very well with ice and strain.

REMEMBER THE FIRST TIME YOU EVER SCORED...a clutch three-pointer in the waning fourth-quarter seconds of a championship basketball game to win one for the home team? Me neither, but I'm sure you were just great!

Safe Sex on the Beach

Chambord Royale
Peach schnapps
Orange juice

STEP 1: Shake 1 part each Chambord and peach schnapps plus a healthy splash of orange juice well with ice.

STEP 2: Strain.

A CONDOM MAY NOT BE NECESSARY to indulge in this liquid verison of sex, but remember, no matter how careful you are, sometimes one thing still leads to another...and it's best to be prepared.

Shotgun Wedding

Buckshot Original Wild West Liqueur

Pour.

LIKE A HOLE IN THE HEAD, for this occasion all you'll need is Buckshot, neat. At just over 100 proof, this spicy shot may be the only thing able to help you forget that the following words could be the last you'll ever hear: "Do you have the ring?"

Purple Haze

Purple haze was in my brain
Lately things don't seem the same.

—**Jimi Hendrix, "Purple Haze"**

Jack Daniel's Tennessee Whiskey
Blue curaçao
Grenadine
Rose's lime juice

Shake 2 parts Jack Daniel's, 1 part blue curaçao, and a dash each of grenadine and Rose's lime juice very well with ice.

SONG LYRICS AS THEY ARE OFTEN SUNG IN BARS: "'Scuse me, while I kiss this guy" (Purple Haze), "You might as well face it, you're a dickhead in love" (Addicted to Love), "She's got electric boobs and a nowhere suit" (Benny and the Jets), "Growin' like a meadow on the engine tonight" (Paradise by the Dashboard Light), "Hang on, Snoopy" (Hang on, Sloopy), "He can't be a man because he doesn't smoke six cigarettes a day" ([I Can't Get No] Satisfaction), "Are you loathsome tonight" (Are You Lonesome Tonight), "Here we are now, we're contagious" (Smells Like Teen Spirit).

Screaming Blue Viking

Would you like the cucumber bruised?

—Woody Boyd to Norm Peterson when Norm orders a Screaming Viking on "Cheers"

Yukon Jack Canadian Liqueur
Aquavit
Blue curaçao

Shake equal parts Yukon Jack and aquavit (Norway's national beverage) plus a splash of blue curaçao very well with ice.

 PATIENCE MAY BE A VIRTUE—especially during the occasional mad dash to the bar for last call—but the ancient Vikings would have none of it. The plea to "keep your shirt on" was coined after a *Berserker* tradition in which Viking warriors would rip their chain mail shirts off in a fury and rush into battle half-naked. *Berserkers* were so named because of their alleged ability to take on the form of bears, so unless you're into that sort of thing, you probably don't want to spend too much time imitating these lunatics.

Bibliography

Durkan, Andrew. *Vendange: A Study of Wine and Other Drinks*. London: Edward Arnold, 1971.

Edwards, Griffith. *Alcohol: The World's Favorite Drug*. New York: St. Martin's Press, 2000.

Elliot, P.T. *100 Proof: Tips and Tales for Spirited Drinkers Everywhere*. New York: Plume, 2000.

Emmons, Bob. *The Book of Tequila: A Complete Guide*. Chicago: Open Court, 1997.

Erdoes, Richard. *Saloons of the Old West*. Avenel, N.J.: Gramercy Books, 1979.

Foley, Ray. *The Ultimate Little Shooter: Book II*. Liberty Corner, N.J.: Foley Publishing, 2000.

Logsdon, Gene. *Good Spirits: A New Look at Ol' Demon Alcohol*. White River Junction, Vt.: Chelsea Green Publishing Company, 1999.

Pacult, F. Paul. *Kindred Spirits: The* Spirit Journal *Guide to the World's Distilled Spirits and Fortified Wines*. New York: Hyperion, 1997.

Weinstein, Bruce. *The Ultimate Party Drink Book*. New York: William Morrow & Co., 2000.

Index